SILVER CLAY WORKSHOP
Getting started in silver clay jewellery

MELANIE BLAIKIE

SILVER CLAY WORKSHOP
Getting started in silver clay jewellery

GUILD OF MASTER CRAFTSMAN PUBLICATIONS

First published 2011 by
Guild of Master Craftsman Publications Ltd
Castle Place, 166 High Street, Lewes, East Sussex BN7 1XU

Text and step-by-step photography © Melanie Blaikie, 2011
Copyright in the Work © GMC Publications Ltd, 2011

ISBN 978-1-86108-832-1

Publisher: Jonathan Bailey
Production Manager: Jim Bulley
Managing Editor: Gerrie Purcell
Senior Project Editor: Virginia Brehaut
Copy Editor: Cath Senker
Managing Art Editor: Gilda Pacitti
Design: Ali Walper
Styled photography: Andrew Perris

Set in Arrus, Freeway and Din
Colour origination by GMC Reprographics
Printed and bound in China by Hing Yip Printing Co. Ltd

CONTENTS

INTRODUCTION

AFTER A CAREER in the London jewellery industry, I decided to move to the country, walk my dogs and make jewellery. I had been a diamond valuer, a stone buyer, designer and jewellery sales consultant but until this point I had not actually made any jewellery myself.

My first attempts at silversmithing were deeply disappointing. After a year, I decided that I had neither the space or financial resources to equip a studio at home nor the time to master all the techniques necessary to create the type of jewellery that I really wanted to make.

Around the same time, I heard about silver metal clay. Although at the time I didn't fully understand what it was, it appeared to be the solution to my problems. I ordered my first packets of silver clay and, since I couldn't find a class or even a book on the subject, I got started on my own. I was hooked immediately. I kept all my equipment in a shoebox and used anything I could find around the house to fashion, shape and texture my clay. Pendants, earrings and even rings soon began to take shape – quickly and easily!

This book is the result of the knowledge I have gained by experimentation, learning, practice and my own teaching experiences. Throughout you will find simple trouble-free projects with clear instructions to re-create at home. If you are a beginner, I hope to show how you can get started with minimal financial outlay by using things you probably already have at home. I have especially designed the projects to be economical, most using 10g or less of silver metal clay (a small packet).

Once you have mastered the basics, you will find exciting projects that introduce more advanced techniques such as ring making, hollow forms and even applying gold leaf.

Have fun with your silver clay!

PROJECT DIFFICULTY RATINGS

Easy projects for beginners that are simple and straightforward to complete even if you have no previous experience of working with metal clay. Minimum equipment or financial outlay needed.

Once you are familiar with the basic techniques, these intermediate projects introduce new skills and require a little more equipment. You will learn how to add colour, texture and fine detail.

These more advanced projects require a higher level of skill and dexterity to create more complex designs. You will learn how to combine several techniques into one piece.

Contrast texture pendant
page 65

Coin bracelet

page 69

Initial pendant

page 73

Forget-me-not earrings

page 77

Textured pendant and earrings

page 81

Lace brooch

page 85

Polymer clay heart pendant
page 89

Porcelain bead necklace

page 93

Classic moulded pendant

page 97

Button cuff links

page 101

Copper-tube beads

page 105

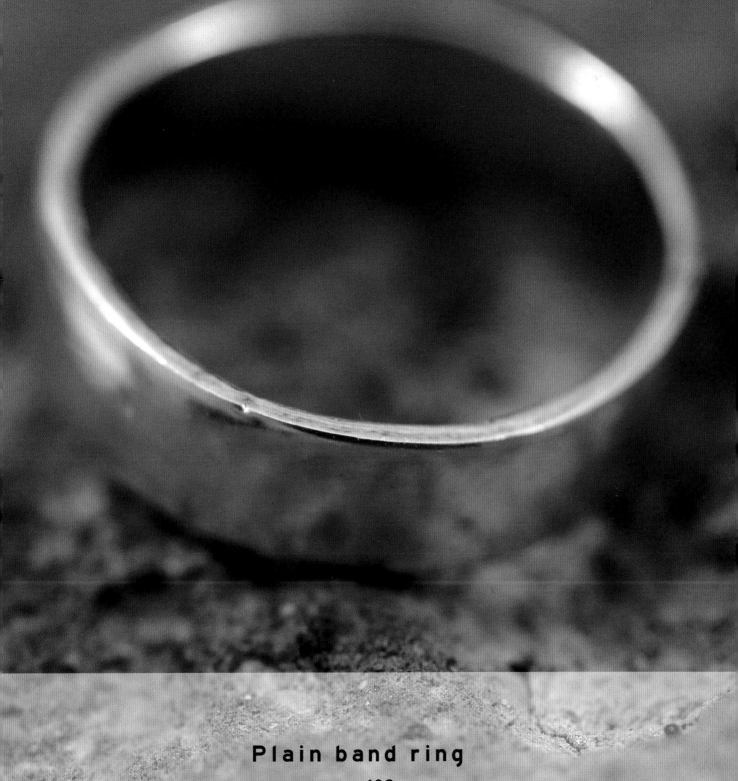

Plain band ring

page 109

Hearts ring

page 113

Cocktail ring

page 117

Enamel pendant

page 121

Linked squares pendant

page 125

Piped ring

page 129

Stacking rings set

page 133

Gold pendant and earrings

page 137

Silver flower moulded bead

page 141

Treble-clef pendant

page 145

Two-part heirloom locket

page 149

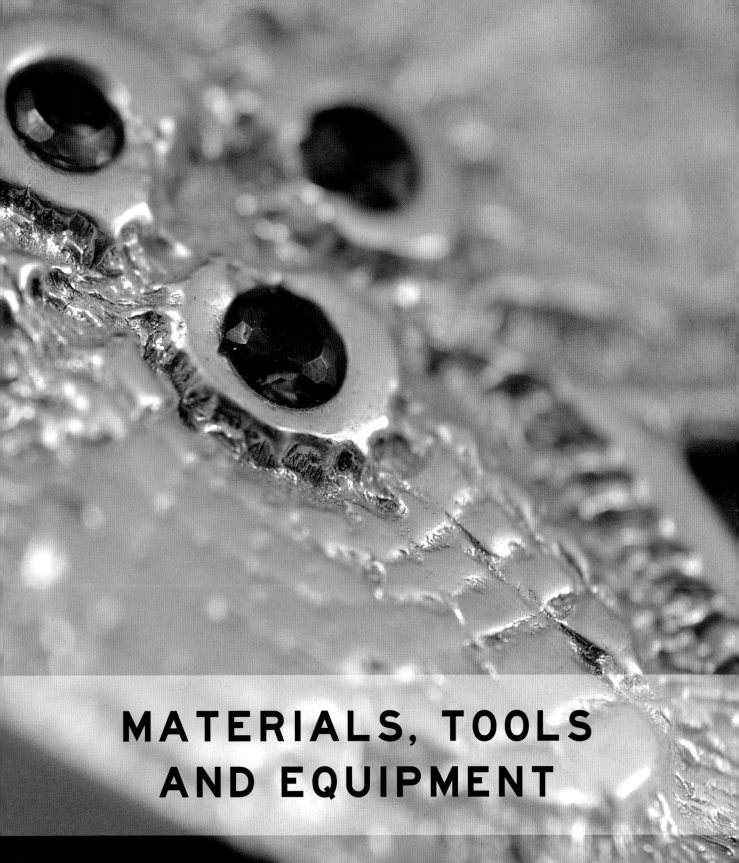

MATERIALS, TOOLS AND EQUIPMENT

What is silver clay?

Silver clay is a truly amazing material – pure silver but in a soft, pliable form that can be easily shaped with fingers and a few simple tools. It seems almost too good to be true but the real beauty of this innovative material is that it allows amateurs to make real silver jewellery at home, without the need for years of technical experience or access to the expensive, specialist equipment used by traditional silversmiths.

BRANDS

There are two main brand names and both have been developed in Japan. Art Clay Silver (ACS) is made by Aida Chemical Industries Company Ltd and Precious Metal Clay (PMC) is manufactured by Mitsubishi Materials Corporation. All of the projects in this book are suitable for both types of clay but do check the manufacturer's instructions for information on firing times, temperatures and shrinkage rates since these can vary. Both brands are sold in grams.

HOW THE SILVER IS MADE

The clay itself is a simple blend of only three natural ingredients: pure silver powder, water and a non-toxic organic binder derived from wood pulp. As well as being a very natural product, the silver powder is recycled silver from the film and photographic industry. The ingredients are mixed to form a very stiff paste or clay-like substance. In the heat of the firing process, the individual particles of silver melt and fuse together; this is called 'sintering' and causes the previously pliable clay to become a solid piece of silver. Once fired, the 'clay' becomes 99.9 per cent pure silver and can be hallmarked 999.

TYPES OF SILVER CLAY

Most of the projects in this book use 'lump'-type silver clay; as the name suggests, this is supplied in an airtight package as a small lump of clay. However, there are also other forms of clay that are fun to experiment with and which can give very different results and effects.

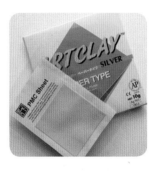

Silver-clay paste or slip

The paste is a watered down 'lump' type. It acts as a glue and is invaluable for joining two pieces of wet or dry clay or for attaching findings. You can buy silver-clay paste ready-made in small pots but it is easy to make yourself. Keep any little leftover pieces of clay that are too small to use in a container, add water and allow the clay to dissolve until you have a smooth, thick paste.

Silver-clay syringe

Silver clay can also be purchased in a syringe with different-sized tips or nozzles to produce lines of varying sizes. Syringed lines can be used to create very effective decorative designs or to position a small amount of clay exactly where needed. The technique for using a syringe is very similar to icing a cake!

Silver-paper type

Although it is called 'paper', this type of silver clay is more like a thick, flexible sheet of dry silver. It can be used very effectively in techniques such as origami or quilling, where folding and creasing are employed. Paper type tends to dissolve if water is added to it and can only be fired in a kiln.

In today's environmentally and cost-conscious climate, silver clay is the perfect product for the amateur jewellery maker to explore and discover!

Tools and equipment for beginners

The first eight projects in this book require a minimum of specialist equipment. You should be able to find most of these items around the house. For a very small financial outlay you can get started and begin to create these easy designs, which you will be proud to wear.

1 Lump clay the most useful form of silver metal clay
2 Silver-clay paste acts as a 'glue' to join two pieces of clay
3 Work mat or surface a clean surface is always required to work from
4 Olive oil to prevent clay from sticking to the work surface

5 Playing cards to use as a work surface and for cutting clay
6 Roller a fat, round marker pen works well if you don't have a roller
7 Sandpaper to create texture
8 Plastic drinking straw to make a neat, round hole

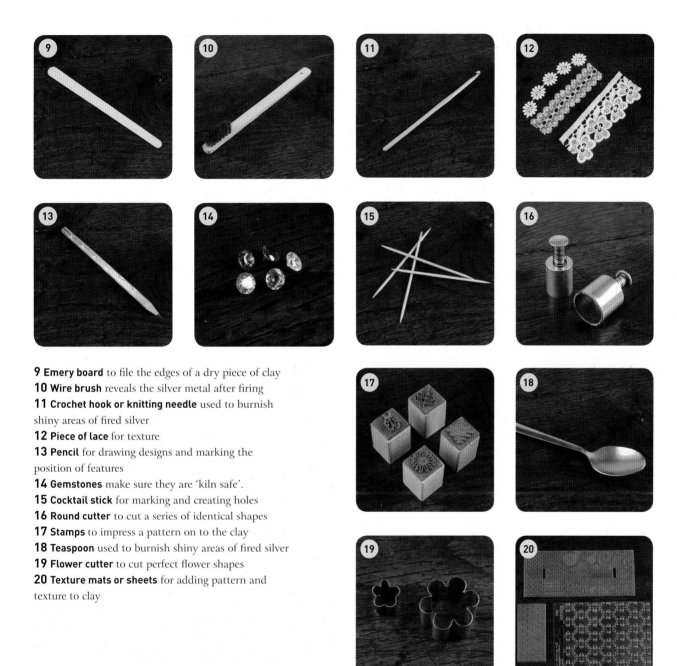

9 **Emery board** to file the edges of a dry piece of clay
10 **Wire brush** reveals the silver metal after firing
11 **Crochet hook or knitting needle** used to burnish shiny areas of fired silver
12 **Piece of lace** for texture
13 **Pencil** for drawing designs and marking the position of features
14 **Gemstones** make sure they are 'kiln safe'.
15 **Cocktail stick** for marking and creating holes
16 **Round cutter** to cut a series of identical shapes
17 **Stamps** to impress a pattern on to the clay
18 **Teaspoon** used to burnish shiny areas of fired silver
19 **Flower cutter** to cut perfect flower shapes
20 **Texture mats or sheets** for adding pattern and texture to clay

21 Heart-shaped cutters an easy way to cut perfect heart shapes

22 Porcelain beads painted with silver clay paste, these beads act as a 'core' for large but inexpensive silver beads

23 Polymer clay useful to practise techniques and as an economical addition to silver clay designs

24 Extra-strong glue to attach fixings that can't be fired or soldered

25 Pliers for joining jump rings

26 Jump rings and clasps for making bracelets

27 Earring fittings sterling-silver earring wire hooks and posts that can be glued or soldered on to the back of earrings

28 Chains, ribbons or thongs for pendants and necklaces

29 Polishing papers papers containing graded particles, which are graded by colour

30 Ceramic tile to provide a smooth work surface for polymer clay

31 Paintbrush for smoothing and shaping clay

32 Syringe silver metal clay supplied in a syringe is great for adding decoration

Intermediate and advanced tools and equipment

Once you have learned the basic techniques, these tools will enable you to complete the remaining projects in this book. Some of these are more specialist items but nearly all will be available from the suppliers listed at the end of this book.

1 Buttons or beads for moulding raid your sewing box or go to a craft store to find unusual designs
2 Bail backs and eyelets neat little fixings made from fine silver that can be attached with paste and fired
3 Copper tubing makes great centres for two-colour beads
4 Ring mandrel a wooden stick to shape rings around

5 Finger-ring gauge cardboard gauge to measure finger size (Japanese sizes)
6 Sticky notepaper very useful to wrap around the mandrel when making rings
7 Sandpaper fine sandpaper can be used to refine dry clay
8 Sponge-backed sanding pad gentle sanding pads for delicate pieces

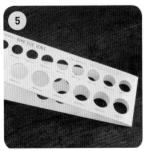

9 Baby wipes great to smooth the surface of flat areas of dry clay

10 Agate burnisher used to shine areas of fired silver and for applying gold leaf

11 Craft knife for cutting clay

12 Rolling strips available in different thicknesses

13 Snake maker, e.g. a flat piece of glass or Perspex; very useful for making thin, even 'snakes' from clay

14 Water spray to add moisture where needed

15 Enamel paints an easy way to add colour to fired silver clay

16 Liver of Sulphur also called Antiquing Solution, this adds an aged patina to fired silver

17 Carving tool for engraving on dry clay

18 Gold foil a very thin leaf of 24-carat gold, which is applied to fired silver with heat and pressure

19 Plastic/Perspex sheet place over a template to make an easy-to-follow design

20 Oblong and square cutters for cutting clay to shape

21 Greaseproof paper to protect gold leaf during cutting

22 Sharp scissors for cutting gold leaf

23 Non-heat-conducting, cross-lock tweezers for holding a silver piece while applying gold leaf

24 Metal pick with a wooden handle for tacking down gold foil

25 Heatproof surface to use when adhering gold leaf to a silver piece

26 Small hand drill or pin vise for drilling holes to hang earrings or a pendant

27 Silver polish for removing coloration when working with Liver of Sulphur

28 Round needle file for making bead holes for a two-part moulded bead

29 Wire cutters for trimming wire

30 Flower and leaf cutters for making decorations

31 Two-part modelling compound for making moulds from found items

32 Cuff-link fittings Sterling-silver fittings that can be glued or soldered on to the front part of the cuff links

materials, tools and equipment

BASIC TECHNIQUES

Planning your design

The aim of this book is to show how easy it can be to design and create silver jewellery. However, even for the simplest design you can save yourself a lot of time, stress and unnecessary cost by taking some time to plan your work before even opening a packet of clay.

The first section of this book contains projects that are ideal for beginners. They require minimal special tools and equipment and have easy-to-follow instructions. If you are new to silver metal clay these are an ideal place for you to begin. You will learn the basic techniques and gain confidence before progressing to the intermediate and advanced projects in later chapters.

1 Where do you look for inspiration? I find it very useful to carry a small notebook so I can jot down ideas or make sketches while I go about my everyday life. Sometimes these might seem rather remote or diverse ideas: a section of a statue in a museum, the handle of an antique spoon, petals of an exotic orchid or the texture of silver-birch bark. They may be nothing to do with jewellery but when I need inspiration, I get out my notebook and all my ideas are there.

2 If the idea of a pencil and paper is a little 'last century' for you, why not embrace technology and collect your ideas electronically? You could snap that gorgeous flower with your mobile phone. Digital cameras are great for recording obscure details that you might notice on holiday or in the city. Create an 'inspiration' file on your computer and refer to it when required.

Once you have an idea, it can be very tempting to rip open a packet of clay and start getting your idea into shape. At this point I would say STOP! Silver metal clay is a precious and expensive resource; it's much better to practise with either play clay or polymer clay. Both are inexpensive materials and behave in a similar way to metal clay. You can test out techniques, decide which tools and equipment will be most useful and even how much silver clay to use, before you move on to the real thing.

3 Play clay is aimed at children: this dough-like clay can be squashed and re-shaped until you are happy with your design.

4 Polymer clay is a soft plastic clay that can be shaped and then baked in a domestic oven to harden and preserve your test designs.

HOW MUCH SILVER CLAY DO I NEED?

All of the projects in this book show how much silver clay is required to complete the design. However, the two main manufacturers supply their clay in packs of differing sizes. This means you can find packs weighing anything from 5g to 50g. Larger packs do tend to be slightly cheaper per gram but this can be a false economy unless you intend to make very large or numerous pieces. Although the clay has a long shelf life, once opened, it begins to dry and becomes less pliable. To begin with, it is sensible to buy two or three smaller packs – 7g or 10g.

Shaping the clay

Silver clay is soft and easy to shape with just a few simple tools.
You'll need to master the techniques of rolling and cutting, either with
cutters or freehand. It is easy to use moulds to shape your clay too.
You may wish to add texture to add sophistication to your designs.

SHAPING WITH FINGERS

1 Using your fingers to shape the clay may seem the easiest and most obvious way to create your designs. However, I have found this not to be the case and would urge caution, especially if you are a beginner. This is because the warmth from your fingers and hands dries the clay, quickly making it become crumbly and less pliable.

2 With practice and by carefully planning your design, it is possible to work directly with your hands but for now, skip this stage and read on.

When you start work, remove from the pack just the amount of clay you need to work with. A light mist of water sprayed into the pack will keep this clay moist while not being used. Wrap clay tightly in a piece of plastic wrap if you intend to leave it for more than a couple of hours.

ROLLING THE CLAY

Most of the projects in this book begin by rolling a thin, flat sheet of clay.

1 A playing card makes an ideal work surface but you may find that the clay has a tendency to stick to it, making it difficult to pick up. Smearing a thin layer of oil over the surface of the playing card will help. Olive oil or any plant-based cooking oil is perfect.

2 Stack five playing cards on either side of the work surface.

3 Roll over the cards and the clay together. This way, you will always roll an even layer of clay to the thickness of the outer stacks of cards. You can use more than five cards, but using fewer than five results in very thin clay, which can be difficult to handle.

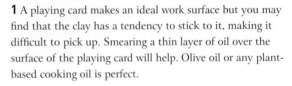

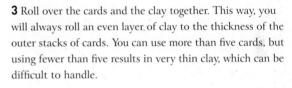

Buy the least expensive playing cards you can find. Good-quality decks have a 'linen' finish but cheap cards have a plastic coating that has better non-stick qualities and is more hard-wearing.

CUTTING SHAPES

There are many tools and specialist devices on the market to help cut designs from your clay.

ADDING PATTERN AND TEXTURE

The easiest way to add pattern, texture, words or letters to your designs is by pressing a stamp or texture into the soft clay.

1 The easiest tool for beginners are these mini cookie-cutters, which are widely available from cook shops, especially those that specialize in cake-decorating supplies. The cutters come in a vast range of shapes and sizes, so you do not need any artistic ability to produce perfect designs.

2 To cut freehand designs from a sheet of clay, you will require a sharp blade such as a tissue blade or a kidney cutter. These work by cutting downwards into the clay, which results in a neat, clean line. Even the long edge of a playing card works well as an improvised cutting tool.

1 Rubber stamps are widely available in a huge variety of designs and patterns. Simply press them on to the soft clay. A slick of oil over the rubber can help if you find the clay is sticking. Stamps can be repeated over a small area to produce an all-over texture or design or they can be specific to the recipient of your jewellery, such as an initial.

2 Texture sheets or texture mats can be made from the same type of rubber as the stamps or they may be clear, embossed sheets of plastic. Simply press them on to the soft clay to reveal amazing patterns or simple outlines. I find an interesting texture can hide a multitude of sins – any fingerprints or unintentional marks simply disappear into the pattern!

MOULDING

Because silver clay is soft and pliable it can easily be pushed into a pre-prepared mould and will assume the shape and any design detail within the mould. Ready-made moulds are available but it is easy and much more fun to make your own.

1 Mix together a two-part modelling compound and press your original object into the soft material. You could use a button, bead, shell or an old earring or brooch. Remove when the modelling material is hardened. There are several versions of this modelling compound on the market. All consist of two colours that harden when mixed. Curing times vary but generally the mould is ready in less than ten minutes.

2 Press silver clay into the mould and dry thoroughly.

3 When the clay is dry it will tip easily out of the mould. Refine any rough edges, affix any necessary loops or rings with silver-clay paste on the back of the piece, and dry again. Fire.

4 Once polished, the silver is an exact replica of the original object.

basic techniques

Drying the clay

As a beginner, it can be very tempting to move quickly from creating your masterpiece in clay to the firing stage, without paying due attention to this important stage of drying. Silver metal clay will dry perfectly well at room temperature. This normally takes at least 24 hours. The warmer and drier your working environment, the faster the clay will dry.

Before firing, the piece needs to be bone-dry because any moisture left in the clay will immediately turn to steam in the heat of the firing process. The steam will expand and force its way out of the clay, which can result in blisters, cracking or even a ruined piece, if it breaks. This can be avoided by thorough drying.

1 To speed up the drying process, small pieces – up to the thickness of five playing cards – can be dried with a hairdryer. Place the piece of clay into a small box, so it doesn't blow away, and give it a good blast with the hairdryer for five minutes on each side. The heat of the hairdryer will not scorch or burn the clay but the air flow might blow it around a bit, so remember to hold on to the box and keep the hairdryer immediately above the piece of clay.

2 Larger pieces benefit from longer, more gentle drying. Pop your finished item on to a ceramic tile or a flat plate and dry in a domestic oven at no more 120° F (50° C) for at least half an hour. Turn the piece over halfway through.

3 An electric food warmer or mug warmer is also excellent for drying clay. Just place the finished piece directly on to the surface, for at least half an hour. Exact times will vary according to the appliance and the thickness of the clay. Turn the piece over halfway through.

4 A craft embossing heat gun dries clay very quickly but has a fierce heat so I find it best to work on a heatproof surface and give four or five short blasts of no more than 15 seconds, turning the piece frequently.

POINTS TO REMEMBER WHEN DRYING:

- Clay gets very hot so be careful when picking up pieces.
- Flat pieces can warp or curl if they dry unevenly; frequent turning can prevent this.
- Appliances vary greatly in temperature so do test and adjust accordingly.
- Even if the clay looks dry on the surface it can be tricky to know if it is completely dry inside – if in doubt, dry some more!
- There is no time limit between the time you make a piece and the time you fire it. If you are short on time, you can leave a finished piece for days or even weeks before it is fired.

Refining dry clay

Once fully dry the clay offers a second opportunity to improve the
design and minimize any small blemishes or mistakes. It is easy
to refine rough or uneven areas and careful attention now can save
time later on. Also, designs can be enhanced by engraving or carving;
now is a good time to drill a neat and tidy hole.

 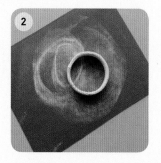  

1 However carefully you have worked at creating your design, uneven or slightly rough edges are difficult to avoid. Feel around the edges of your piece. Any roughness that you can feel now will make the finished piece uncomfortable to wear. Gentle filing with an emery board is often all that is needed to smooth the edges of a flat or simple piece of unfired clay. Support the piece well between your fingers and avoid applying undue pressure, which could cause it to break.

2 Larger areas, such as the flat edges of a ring or the back of a pendant, can be easily smoothed by placing the piece flat on to a sheet of fine sandpaper. Move the piece gently over the paper in circles to flatten and smooth any areas in contact with the surface.

3 Very delicate pieces respond well to being smoothed with sponge-backed sanding pads. These are a gentle form of sandpaper on a sponge backing, which can be cut to size and folded to fit into small spaces like the inside of a ring. A fine-grade sanding pad is an excellent dry finishing treatment for areas that will be polished to a smooth and shiny finish after firing.

4 Engraving is a more advanced technique for adding pattern to the clay once it is completely dry. Draw the design on to the dry clay with a pencil before you begin. Use a scribing tool or a sharp-tipped burnisher to follow the design and create the first, shallow line.

Dry clay is often referred to as being in a plaster-
or chalk-like state. Both are accurate in describing
how fragile and brittle the dry clay is before firing.
This makes the refining process easy but means you
need to work very gently and carefully at this stage.

5 A sharp, V-shaped carving tool can then be used to add depth to the line. When fired, this technique produces clean lines and crisp detail.

6 If you have a small hand drill, or pin vise, and a steady hand it is possible to drill holes into the clay at this stage. Mark the position of the hole first with a pencil. Avoid pushing down on to the fragile clay; work slowly and let the weight of the drill do the work. This results in a neat, clean hole.

7 Working with silver-metal clay, I find it is almost impossible to make a mistake that cannot be rectified by some means! If the worst happens and a piece breaks at this stage, it is usually possible to mend it by pasting the pieces back together with silver-clay paste.

8 Align the broken edges and apply a good, thick layer of paste over the join. Allow to dry and repeat. If you work on the back of the piece, the join should be almost invisible from the front once it is fired.

Firing the clay

There are three ways to fire silver clay. The method you choose may depend upon what equipment you already have at home, how much money you want to spend and how far along your silver clay journey you have travelled. The good news is that all methods are very easy!

FIRING ON A GAS RING

I am covering this method first since it is probably the easiest and requires hardly anything more than the gas hob you already have in your kitchen. If you don't have a gas hob, one of those simple butane-gas stoves used by campers works equally well and the technique is exactly the same.

   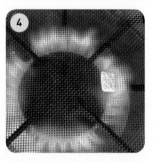

1 To support your finished pieces while they fire you will need a piece of metal mesh, which is placed directly over the gas ring, resting on the hob.

2 When the gas is lit, the flame will heat parts of the mesh until they glow bright orange. These 'hot spots' are where you place your dried, finished pieces of clay to fire.

3 Reduce the flame and using tweezers, place the items to be fired on to one of the hot spots.

4 Increase the flame to the hottest setting and leave the items to fire for five minutes. After five minutes, turn the flame off and allow them to cool. I have found that leaving items for longer than five minutes has no adverse affect, making this the ideal firing method to coincide with a tea break. But don't forget to keep an eye on what's happening on the hob!

FIRING WITH A KITCHEN TORCH

Sometimes called a chef's or brûlé torch, this is a quick and easy way to fire. In addition to the torch, you will also need a good, heatproof surface to fire on. I use a ceramic fibre brick, which provides a flat firing area and protects the work surface.

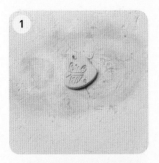

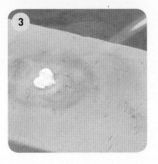

1 Place the item to be fired on to the brick and light the torch. With this method of firing, the temperature of the silver is controlled by the distance of the flame. Begin by warming the piece gently from approx. 8–10in (20–25cm) distance, keeping the torch moving slowly in small circles so as to heat the piece evenly.

2 Bringing the flame towards the silver 1–2in (2½–5cm) at a time will cause the silver to become hotter until it begins to glow a bright, peachy orange colour. When this colour is achieved, the metal has reached the correct temperature and the firing process can begin. Keep the torch moving and at the same distance to the silver, maintaining the correct temperature for two minutes. Turn off the torch and allow the silver to cool.

3 During the firing process, the binder material burns off; when the torch is firing, it is often possible to see this happening. When the binder burns it causes a small amount of smoke and a tiny blue flame, which lasts only for a few seconds. If you see this, don't worry, it's part of the firing process and is over in seconds.

I have found it is possible to overheat the silver with a torch, causing the surface to melt. However, by watching closely this is easy to avoid. If the colour of the metal exceeds the 'peachy orange' state, moves towards red and the surface begins to look liquid, the silver is too hot. Reduce the heat quickly by moving the torch back just an inch or two (2½–5cm) and continue.

KILN FIRING

A kiln is best for firing larger pieces that may be difficult to heat evenly using either of the above two methods or if you have lots of pieces to fire at one time. Also, if you are interested in exploring techniques such as glass fusing in the future, it may be worth investing in a kiln.

1 Many electric kilns have computerized programmes, making it easy to heat or cool the kiln at different rates as well as to maintain pre-set temperatures. Most can be used with a domestic plug socket.

2 All brands of silver metal clay come with detailed kiln-firing instructions, which should be referred to. However, almost without exception, the firing schedules are quick and easy. My kiln heats to firing temperature in less than half an hour, and the actual firing takes less than ten minutes.

Always place items to be fired on a shelf in the kiln and never directly on the floor. Arrange multiple pieces so that they are not touching. Use long tongs and heatproof gloves when placing the shelf into the kiln or removing after firing.

FIRING GUIDELINES

ART CLAY 650	GAS HOB	TORCH	KILN
Firing time	5 mins	2–2½ mins	1,200°F (650°C) – 30 mins 1,290°F (700°C) – 20 mins 1,450°F (800°C) – 8 mins
Size limit	Maximum size: 2 x 1¼ x ¾in (5 x 3 x 2cm) Up to 1oz (25g)	Maximum diameter of 1½in (4cm) Up to 1oz (25g)	Depends on size
Remarks	Easy, low cost, suitable for most jewellery size pieces	Involves a flame, but quick and easy with practice	Very easy, no guess work, especially good for large or multiple items

Polishing and finishing

At last, your piece of clay begins to look like real silver! At this stage, the full beauty and brilliant white shine of the finished metal can be revealed. Because you are now working with silver metal, these techniques are comparable to traditional silversmithing skills but all can be easily achieved at home with a few simple tools.

1 After firing, at first it can be disappointing to see that your piece of silver still has a matt, white surface and looks very much like unfired clay. This white surface is just unpolished silver and can be quickly dealt with. Brush firmly over the surface of the whole piece with a wire brush. Almost immediately a satiny, silver shine is revealed – a real ooh-ahhh moment!

2 Some areas, such as the inside of a ring, can be more difficult to reach. A short bristled brush is ideal where space is tight.

The semi-matt, satin finish that brushing reveals is very attractive and many silver-clay artists, both beginners and professional, prefer to leave their designs at this stage. However, there are several ways to continue the polishing process and achieve a glossy, mirror-like shine.

3 Burnishing requires only one or two simple tools and is easy to do at home. An inexpensive stainless steel teaspoon makes a great burnishing tool. Rub hard over the surface of the silver with a smooth part of the teaspoon; either the bowl or curved end of the handle. The great thing about burnishing is that the more you work at it, the better the result, so keep at it!

4 Burnishing works best on flat areas but if you want to pick out part of your design, a metal crochet hook or knitting needle also makes a great burnisher. If your piece is flat, such as this pendant, don't forget to burnish around the edges. Even if you decide to leave it at the semi-matt stage, burnished edges give a hint of sparkle and a professional finish. It is also possible to soften the edges of a corner to a bevel with a burnisher.

5 One of my favourite tools is my agate burnisher. The grey tip of this stick is made from agate, which is a very hard stone. It works beautifully over smooth and textured surfaces.

Burnishing works by flattening the surface of the fired silver. The flatter and smoother the surface, the better it will reflect the light and the shinier it will appear. Any smooth object that has a harder surface than the silver – which is relatively soft – can be used as a burnisher. Experiment with the tools shown here to find the one that works best for your design.

basic techniques

59

6 Sponge-backed sanding pads have a gritty surface on a soft, spongy backing and can be used on dry or fired clay. To polish up fired silver, wire-brush first and begin with the roughest (or largest) grit. Work thoroughly over the surface of the entire piece for at least ten minutes. Then move to the next finest grit and repeat. Continue working through the grits to the finest grade. The silver should now have a deep mirror-like shine.

7 Polishing papers also contain graded particles but these are almost invisible. The papers are graded by colours. Follow the manufacturer's instructions to work through the colours in the correct order. Papers can be folded to get into awkward nooks and crannies such as the inside of rings.

8 By now, you should be able to see if you were diligent enough at the previous stage of refining the dry clay. To achieve a true mirror finish, the pre-firing stages of sanding and smoothing the surface are key. Unfortunately, the smooth, polished surface highlights any tiny imperfections. The only way to remove these now is by using a metal file. The lesson here is that a few minutes' care at the refining stage can save hours of hard work later.

9 The only electrical polishing device I have used in this book is my barrel polisher (also known as a tumble polisher). Widely available from craft or jewellery suppliers, this polisher can save time if you have lots of pieces to polish.

Whether you choose to burnish your fired piece or work through the grades of sanding pads or polishing papers, it is easy and satisfying to achieve a lovely finish. For super-shiny results, use a combination of methods, finishing with the finest grade of paper and buff with silver polish.

10 The barrel polisher is similar to those used for polishing stones but the medium used for polishing silver is called metal 'shot' – thousands of tiny pieces of smooth, stainless steel which tumble around as the barrel rotates and polish the silver. This method produces an even shine and is great for dealing with unusually shaped pieces. If you have hollow shapes such as beads to polish, thread them first on to a piece of string or wire to prevent the shot becoming trapped inside the bead.

11 To finish the polishing process, a dab of commercial silver polish applied with a soft cloth will make your silver glow.

Fired silver clay is almost completely pure silver and does not contain the copper element that is responsible for 'normal' silver tarnishing. Hence, your silver clay jewellery will require very little cleaning. If it does start to look dull, any of the proprietary silver-cleaning solutions will restore its shine. A quick wipe over with a silver polishing cloth every now and then will keep it sparkling.

THE PROJECTS

Contrast texture pendant

This abstract design pendant is one of the quickest and easiest pieces I have ever made. You don't need any special equipment – you should be able to find everything you need to create this pendant around the house. It's amazing that a rough piece of sandpaper can produce such a sophisticated finish.

MATERIALS

- 10g pack of silver metal clay
- Olive oil
- Playing cards
- Roller
- Piece of rough-grade sandpaper
- Plastic drinking straw
- Emery board
- Wire brush
- Crochet hook or knitting needle
- Satin cord or ribbon to finish

STEP ONE Set up the work area using one playing card as a work surface and stack five playing cards on either side. These outer stacks act as rolling guides and will help you to roll the clay into a thin, even layer. Smear a tiny amount of oil on to the central card; this acts as a release agent and will make it much easier to pick up the clay later. Place 10g of silver clay on to the central card. Using a mini rolling pin (or even a fat, round pen) gently roll across the clay to reduce the thickness until the clay is the same thickness as the five cards on the outside and you can roll no further.

STEP TWO Remove the outer stacks of cards. Lay a strip of sandpaper on either side of the clay and roll it again, gently but firmly, over the paper. The clay will change shape slightly.

STEP THREE Carefully peel away the sandpaper strips to reveal the rough texture underneath.

STEP FOUR Make a hole at the top of the pendant using a piece of plastic drinking straw and cut out a neat circle. Dry the piece thoroughly. You don't need to remove the clay from the playing card in order to dry it. As the clay dries, it will automatically release itself from the card.

STEP FIVE Once dry, the clay has a brittle, chalky texture and can easily break. Working very carefully, gently file around the edges of the pendant with an emery board. For this design, I like to maintain some of the natural, uneven edges and abstract shape, so no need to file until perfectly smooth. However, do ensure that any really rough or sharp areas are smoothed or the pendant won't be comfortable to wear.

Don't worry if the clay doesn't roll out to an even, oval shape. The unusual, abstract shapes that occur by accident at this stage can be most attractive and will make your pendant unique.

STEP SIX Fire the pendant. Allow to cool completely before continuing.

STEP SEVEN After firing, the pendant is solid silver. Brush the surface firmly with a wire brush. Very quickly, you will see that as the surface begins to smooth, a lovely silvery shine appears. Brush the front and back of the pendant and don't forget the edges!

STEP EIGHT The eye-catching design of this pendant is created by leaving the textured sides at the brushed stage and burnishing the central smooth panel. Carefully burnish the central strip by rubbing hard over the surface with a burnishing tool such as a crochet hook or a knitting needle. This will create a high shine. Also, burnish around the outer edges of the pendant for added sparkle.

STEP NINE The satin cord can easily be pushed through the hole to complete the pendant and gives a sophisticated finish.

Work in different directions to minimize any marks made by the burnishing tool. Be careful not to stray over into the textured sections, which could spoil the design.

contrast texture pendant

Coin bracelet

It's not easy to make a bracelet without using lots of clay but this lovely project achieves it with just one 10g pack! The 'coins' are cut from a sheet of clay with circular, mini-cookie cutters. These are widely available from craft and cake-decorating shops and are definitely worth the investment.

MATERIALS

- 10g pack of silver metal clay
- Olive oil
- Playing cards
- Roller
- Round cutter approx. ¾in (2cm) diameter
- Cocktail stick
- Smooth-sided mug or glass
- Emery board
- Wire brush
- Pliers
- Jump rings
- Clasp

STEP ONE Lightly oil a playing card; this will be your work surface. Stack five playing cards on either side of the work surface and roll the silver clay to a flat, even layer.

STEP TWO Use the cutter to cut out as many rounds as possible. You should be able to pick up and peel away the excess clay from around the circles without disturbing the 'coins'.

STEP THREE Combine the scraps from step two, oil a fresh playing card and re-roll them between two stacks of five cards, as in step one. The texture of the clay will be slightly less smooth this time but don't worry about fine lines or an uneven surface texture – it adds to the character of your coins! Re-roll the scraps again until there is no clay left. I made eight coins from my 10g pack of silver clay.

STEP FOUR Carefully remove the coins from their cards and move them on to the side of a mug to dry. This gives the coins a gentle curve so the finished bracelet fits more comfortably around the wrist. With a cocktail stick, first mark and then create the small holes for the rings that will later join the coins. When the coins are completely dry, they will slip easily off the surface of the mug.

To pick a clay shape up from the card without distorting its shape, gently bend the playing card backwards and the edge of the clay will lift enough to allow you to carefully remove it from the card.

STEP FIVE When dry, the clay has a dry, chalky feel and is very brittle. Working very carefully, gently file around each coin with the emery board to smooth any rough or uneven edges.

STEP SIX Fire the coins using your chosen method. Here, I used a camping-gas stove so I could fire them all at once!

STEP SEVEN Vigorously brush the coins with your wire brush to bring up a satiny, silver shine. I could burnish or polish the coins at this stage but I've decided not to because I really like the contrast with the polished rings when the bracelet is made up.

STEP EIGHT Use a pair of pliers to join the coins with jump rings. Then add as many extra rings as you need to make your bracelet the correct length before adding the clasp.

coin bracelet

Initial pendant

This is a lovely project that is easy to complete with just a few bits and pieces, which you should be able to find in your kitchen drawer or craft box. These pendants make great presents since they can be personalized, and you should be able to make two or three from a 7g pack of clay.

MATERIALS

- 7g pack of silver metal clay
- Olive oil
- Playing cards
- Roller
- Round cutter ⅔in (1½cm) diameter
- Cocktail stick
- Initial stamps
- Emery board
- Wire brush
- Teaspoon
- Pliers
- Jump ring
- Chain
- Extra gemstones, beads or pearls (optional)

STEP ONE Lightly oil a playing card; this will be your work surface. Stack five playing cards on either side of the work surface and roll the silver clay to a flat, even layer.

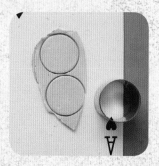

STEP TWO Use a small, round cutter to cut out two circles and then carefully peel away the excess clay from around the edges to reveal the two discs. The excess should come away quite easily if you have lightly oiled the card.

STEP THREE Use a cocktail stick to make a small hole at the top of each circle. You might like to make a small pin-point indent with the tip of the cocktail stick first and check that the hole is going to be exactly where you want it. This is a very easy way to make a hole, without having to pick up the clay. Don't worry if your hole looks a little ragged or uneven; you can improve and refine it later.

STEP FOUR Carefully line up the initial stamp and press firmly but gently on to the surface of the clay. Now set the card aside until the clay has dried completely. If you dry the clay on the playing card, it will release itself from the surface as it dries.

If your cutters are open backed, like mine, you may find it easier to stamp the initial on to the clay and then cut around it. I find that making the hole first helps me to place the initial correctly since it doesn't need to go in the centre of the circle.

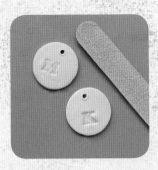 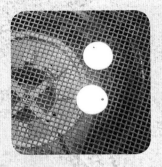  

STEP FIVE When the clay is absolutely bone-dry it has a brittle, chalky texture and can easily break or snap. Working very carefully, use an emery board to gently file around the edges of the discs to smooth any rough edges. You can also work over the area around the hole to file away any unevenness.

STEP SIX When the clay is completely dry and you have made any refinements necessary, your piece is now ready to fire. Here, the shapes are being fired on a camping-gas ring.

STEP SEVEN To reveal the silver, brush the surface with a wire brush. After just a few strokes with the brush, the discs turn from matt white to satiny silver.

STEP EIGHT The polishing process can now be continued in a number of ways. However, one of the easiest ways to achieve a nice shine without any specialist tools is to burnish the surface with a teaspoon! Both the handle and the bowl of a teaspoon make good burnishing tools. Rub them firmly over the surface of the silver and the initial. By working in different directions you can minimize any lines left by the burnisher and the more you work at it, the shinier the silver will become. It still amazes me how the silver can be transformed at this stage with a tool as simple as a teaspoon!

STEP NINE The silver initial disc is now ready to be added to the necklace. Use pliers to fix on a jump ring and a chain. I've added some extra gems to make the necklace really special but you could also use glass beads, pearls or coloured gemstones.

initial pendant

75

Forget-me-not earrings

These pretty feminine earrings are quick and easy to make and need so little
clay that they can be made from the scraps left over from another project.
If you have enough, you could make a couple of pairs and have them
ready in case you need a birthday gift in a hurry!

MATERIALS

- 5g pack of silver metal clay
- Olive oil
- Playing cards
- Roller
- Small flower cutter approx. ½in (1cm) diameter
- Cocktail stick
- Emery board
- Wire brush
- Crochet hook or knitting needle
- Earring posts
- Extra-strong glue

STEP ONE Lightly oil a playing card to provide your work surface. Stack five playing cards on either side of the work surface and roll the silver clay to a flat, even layer.

STEP TWO Use a very small flower cutter to cut out the forget-me-nots for the earrings.

STEP THREE Carefully peel away the excess clay to reveal the flower shapes.

STEP FOUR With a cocktail stick, mark the centre of the flower and then use the tip of the stick to impress the marks of the petals. Dry the flowers on the playing card; as they dry, they will automatically release themselves from the card.

STEP FIVE Gently file around the edges of the shapes with an emery board.

STEP SIX Fire the flower shapes. Here I have used mesh over a camping-gas ring.

STEP SEVEN Brush the flowers with a wire brush to bring up a silver shine.

STEP EIGHT Burnish the flowers by rubbing firmly over the surface with a burnishing tool such as a crochet hook or knitting needle. This will bring up a bright shine.

STEP NINE Attach earring posts on to the back of the flowers, see tip below.

Throughout this book, where I have used sterling silver fittings such as these earring posts, these can easily be soldered on to your fine silver designs if you have the skill and the equipment to do so. If not, an extra-strong glue, which is suitable for metals, is a simpler alternative method of joining the two pieces.

Textured pendant and earrings

This matching set of pendant and earrings is made by applying
an interesting texture decoration to the clay. Useful textures are all
around us, and for this project you can use either bought or found textures.
Although I have chosen round cutters, this project would work equally
well with a set of heart-shaped or square cutters.

MATERIALS

- 10g pack of silver metal clay
- Olive oil
- Playing cards
- Roller
- Clear plastic textured sheet, lace, rubber texture mat or other object to create texture
- Large round cutter 1½in (4cm), medium round cutter ¾in (2cm), small round cutter ³⁄₁₆in (5mm) diameter
- Emery board
- Wire brush
- Crochet hook or knitting needle
- Earring-wire hooks
- Pliers
- Jump rings
- Suede thong or a ribbon

STEP ONE Lightly oil a playing card; this will be your work surface. Stack five playing cards on either side of the work surface and roll the silver clay to a flat, even layer.

STEP TWO Press your chosen texture firmly on to the surface of the clay.

STEP THREE Using the largest circle cutter, cut out the pendant. Remove the excess clay and keep covered and moist until needed.

The most popular way to create texture is to use a rubber texture mat. Note that this requires a light coating of oil to prevent it from sticking.

STEP FOUR Use the medium round cutter to cut a circle from the upper part of the pendant. This will create both the hole for hanging the pendant and the circle for the first earring.

STEP FIVE Carefully move the pendant on to another card, leaving the circle for the earring on the original card. Using the smallest round cutter, cut another circle from the top of the earring. Save this smallest circle with the other spare clay.

STEP SIX Roll out all the remaining clay as in step one and apply texture. Cut a second medium circle for the second earring and another small circle, as before, for hanging the earring. Dry all three pieces thoroughly.

STEP SEVEN When the clay is completely dry, carefully file the edges with an emery board to smooth any roughness.

STEP EIGHT Fire the finished pieces by your chosen method and according to the manufacturer's instructions. I have used mesh over a camping-gas ring.

STEP NINE Brush the fired silver firmly with a wire brush to bring up the silver shine.

Save any excess clay for your next project or use it to add extra decoration to the pendant and earrings.

STEP TEN Burnish the pendant and earrings by rubbing firmly over the surface with a burnishing tool such as a crochet hook or knitting needle. This will bring up a bright shine.

STEP ELEVEN Make up the finished pieces. Attach earring-wire hooks using pliers to attach the jump rings. Thread a piece of thong or ribbon through the pendant for a modern look.

textured pendant and earrings

Lace brooch

A scrap of lace can make a surprisingly beautiful texture.
Test out different types and patterns of lace by rolling them on to a piece
of modelling clay first. Choose your favourite pattern to work with before
opening the silver clay. This project could work equally well as a pendant.

MATERIALS

- 10g pack of silver metal clay
- Olive oil
- Playing cards
- Roller
- Piece of lace
- Pencil
- Tissue blade (optional)
- 3 or 4 man-made gemstones such as cubic zirconia
- Cocktail stick
- Emery board
- Wire brush
- Crochet hook or knitting needle
- Burnishing tool
- Brooch fitting
- Extra-strong glue

STEP ONE Lightly oil a playing card; this will be your work surface. Stack five playing cards on either side of the work surface and roll the silver clay to a flat, even layer.

STEP TWO Place your chosen piece of lace on top of the clay and roll again. This will press the lace into the silver clay, creating an imprint of the pattern.

STEP THREE Carefully peel back the lace to reveal the pattern.

STEP FOUR Trim the edges of the clay into a pleasing shape. This might follow a pattern suggested by the lace imprint or it could be a completely abstract shape – whatever you think looks good. You could use a tissue blade if you have one; the edge of a playing card also makes a good cutting tool.

STEP FIVE Before adding the stones, it helps to make small indents with the tip of a pencil where the stones will sit. Make sure you choose a part of the pattern where the thickness of the clay is at least equal to the depth of the stones to be used.

STEP SIX Drop the pointed end of each stone into the prepared hole and push gently into place with a cocktail stick. It is important that the widest part of the stone – the girdle – is firmly embedded in the clay. If too much of the stone sits above the surface of the clay, it will fall out when the piece is fired. Allow the piece to dry completely.

STEP SEVEN If the stones have been placed correctly, they will be almost invisible when the piece is viewed edge on.

STEP EIGHT Once dry, the clay becomes brittle and chalky. It is very easy to break the piece at this stage so work very carefully and gently. Tidy up and smooth any rough or uneven edges by filing gently with an emery board.

STEP NINE Fire the brooch. The brooch could be fired in a kiln or with a cook's torch but here I have used mesh over a camping-gas ring. Allow the piece to cool naturally. Cooling too quickly may cause the stones to shatter due to thermal shock.

STEP TEN Brush the brooch firmly with a wire brush to bring up the silver shine.

STEP ELEVEN The silver can now be polished with a burnishing tool. Professional burnishing tools can be made from stainless steel or agate but I find a metal crochet hook or knitting needle works equally well and can get into the fine lines of the lace pattern.

STEP TWELVE Use the extra-strong glue to fix the brooch bar on to the back of the piece. Alternatively, if you have the means to do so (and your brooch bar is also silver), you could solder the two together.

lace brooch

Polymer clay heart pendant

How can you make a tiny scrap of silver clay look a lot more than it really is? Add some inexpensive polymer clay and you will have a beautiful pendant. This technique introduces plenty of scope for incorporating different shapes, styles and colours. Why not experiment and make one for every outfit?

MATERIALS

- 5g of silver metal clay
- Olive oil
- Playing cards
- A pair of matching heart-shaped cutters: large approx. 1½in (4cm) long and small approx. ⅔in (1½cm)
- Roller
- Emery board
- Polishing papers
- Burnisher
- Smooth surface such as a ceramic tile
- Polymer clay
- Kitchen plastic wrap
- Piece of drinking straw
- Extra-strong glue
- Suede thong, ribbon or chain

STEP ONE Lightly oil a playing card to be your work surface. Roll some small scraps of silver clay between two stacks of five playing cards. Use the smaller cutter to cut out the silver heart. Remove any excess clay and save. Dry the heart.

STEP TWO Carefully file the heart, smoothing any uneven edges.

STEP THREE Fire the heart by your chosen method and according to the manufacturer's instructions.

This project would work equally well with two squares, two circles or two oblong cutters.

STEP FOUR The silver heart can be highly polished to contrast with the matt finish of the red polymer clay. Use polishing papers and a burnisher to achieve this effect.

STEP FIVE Working on a smooth surface such as a ceramic tile, soften the polymer clay by rolling and folding it several times. Roll the polymer clay to a thickness of approximately ¼in (5mm) – the depth of about 15 playing cards.

STEP SIX Press the finished silver heart lightly into the centre of the polymer clay. Cover your work with a sheet of kitchen plastic wrap. With the larger cutter, press down on the plastic film and cut through the polymer clay. This flattens the silver heart into the polymer clay and creates a soft, rounded edge to the larger polymer shape.

STEP SEVEN Make a hole in the pendant with a drinking straw. Now bake the whole pendant, without moving the silver heart, according to the polymer clay manufacturer's instructions. Polymer clay can be baked in a conventional domestic oven at a low temperature. Allow to cool.

STEP EIGHT Carefully remove the silver heart, place a couple of drops of extra-strong glue into the hole and replace the silver heart.

STEP NINE Finish the pendant with your choice of chain, ribbon or thong.

polymer clay heart pendant

Porcelain bead necklace

The porcelain beads used as the base for this dramatic necklace
come in many different shapes and sizes. This is a very economical
way of creating large beads and is particularly suitable when
several beads of the same weight and dimensions are needed.
The beads can be decorated in a variety of ways.

MATERIALS

- 10g silver-clay paste
- Several porcelain bead bases
- Cocktail sticks
- Small paintbrush
- Scraps of silver metal clay (optional)
- Syringe for making patterns (optional)
- Wire brush
- Crochet hook or knitting needle
- Ribbon
- Pliers
- Clasp
- Small bead or pearl

STEP ONE Support the base bead on a cocktail stick so that it is easy to hold while painting. Paint the first layer of silver-clay paste over the porcelain base and allow it to dry. Repeat the painting process another four times.

STEP TWO There are a hundred and one ways to decorate your bead once you have completed five layers of painted paste. Small scraps of clay from earlier projects can be used to make shapes or cut-outs, which can be pressed on to the last layer while still wet. Random lines or patterns created with a syringe also look good. Here, I have made my fifth or last layer of paste very thick and textured it with the tip of a cocktail stick.

STEP THREE Fire the beads. It is easy to fire them in a kiln. If you use a gas ring, turn the beads after five minutes and fire for a further five minutes. Cool completely.

Due to the size and thickness of the beads, firing them with a kitchen torch is not suitable since it is very difficult to heat the silver evenly.

STEP FOUR Brush firmly with a wire brush to bring out the silver shine and the beauty of the texture.

STEP FIVE Burnish over the rough surface using a crochet hook or knitting needle and the beads will really sparkle!

STEP SIX A contrasting piece of dark ribbon makes a dramatic setting for these spectacular beads. Finish with clasp ends and a small bead or pearl to complete.

porcelain bead necklace

Classic moulded pendant

Making a mould from a favourite bead, button or shell is great fun
and very easy. The same technique can be applied to a wide variety of
original items and the results are quite spectacular! It is also useful when
several identical components are needed, such as for a necklace.

MATERIALS

- Two-part modelling compound
- A playing card
- An interesting bead, button or original object
- 7g pack of silver metal clay
- Sandpaper
- Emery board
- Silver-clay paste
- A bail back (ready-made loop of fine silver)
- Fine silver loop
- Cocktail stick
- Wire brush
- Crochet hook or knitting needle
- Liver of Sulphur
- Chain with clasp

STEP ONE Measure equal amounts of a two-part modelling compound. The two colours stay soft and easy to handle until mixed together, when the curing or hardening process will begin.

STEP TWO Knead the two parts together in your hands until the colour is uniform with no marbling or visible streaks. Shape the compound into roughly the shape of the item to be moulded. You will need to work quite quickly at this stage.

STEP THREE Press the object (here a carved bead) into the moulding compound. Make sure that the edges of the compound are pressed firmly and snugly up to the edge of the bead or whatever object you are using. This will ensure that the 'walls' of your mould are straight with defined corners.

STEP FOUR When the moulding compound has set firm – refer to manufacturers' instructions for timings – the object can be removed from the mould.

STEP FIVE This is the easy bit! Press the silver clay into your mould. This bead mould used 7g of clay but you may need to adjust the amount according to the size of your own mould.

STEP SIX When the silver clay is completely dry it will easily tip out of the mould. The drying stage may take longer than you would normally expect because there is little opportunity for air to circulate around the clay when it is in the mould.

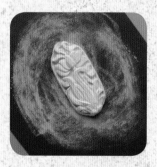

STEP SEVEN It will help later on if the back of the pendant is quite flat. Place the dry piece of clay, back downwards, on to a piece of sandpaper and move it around gently in a figure of eight pattern until the back is smoothed. It doesn't need to be completely flat.

STEP EIGHT Carefully work around the edges of your clay shape with an emery board to smooth any rough edges.

STEP NINE To hang the pendant, you can attach a bail back. First, apply two small blobs of silver-clay paste to the back of the piece. Then place the loop over the paste.

STEP TEN Apply a generous blob of silver-clay paste over each foot of the loop so that it will be firmly attached to the body of the pendant. The easiest way to move small amounts of paste is with a cocktail stick. Dry and repeat as necessary until the feet are well covered. Ensure the piece is completely dry and fire by your chosen method and according to the manufacturer's instructions.

STEP ELEVEN Brush the fired silver firmly with a wire brush to bring up a matt silver shine. Then rub firmly over the surface with a burnishing tool such as a crochet hook or knitting needle. This will bring up a bright shine. The pendant here has also been lightly 'aged' with a solution of Liver of Sulphur (see page 40), to highlight the contrast between the raised and recessed areas of the design.

Small ready-made fittings or 'findings' of fine silver can be added directly to the unfired clay and safely fired as one piece. Sterling-silver findings are best added after firing since the heat will cause a black layer of firescale to form, which must be removed before work can continue.

STEP TWELVE The pendant is hung on a chain threaded through the loop on the back. This gives an 'invisible' attachment so that the pendant appears to be floating on the chain.

classic moulded pendant

99

Button cuff links

An ideal present for the man in your life or a great gift for Father's Day. Using the moulding technique, a pair of simple buttons are transformed into stylish cuff links. You could choose a more decorative style of button or add gemstones to create a pair for more glitzy evening wear.

MATERIALS

- Two-part modelling compound
- A playing card
- Two buttons
- 7g pack of silver metal clay
- Sandpaper
- Emery board
- Fine-grain sponge-backed sanding pads
- Wire brush
- Crochet hook or knitting needle
- Cuff-link fittings
- Extra-strong glue

STEP ONE Measure equal amounts of a two-part modelling compound. The two colours stay soft and easy to handle until mixed together, when the curing or hardening process will begin.

STEP TWO Knead the two parts together in your hands until the colour is uniform with no marbling or visible streaks. Shape the compound into a rough 'sausage' shape and press in the buttons. You will need to work quite quickly at this stage. Make sure that the edges of the compound are pressed firmly and snugly up to the edge of the buttons. This will ensure that the 'walls' of your mould are straight with defined corners.

STEP THREE When the moulding compound has set firm – refer to the manufacturer's instructions for timings – the buttons can be removed from the mould.

STEP FOUR Divide 7g of silver clay into two. Press half of the silver clay firmly into each button mould and dry thoroughly. The drying stage may take longer than you would normally expect because there is little opportunity for air to circulate around the clay when it is in the mould.

STEP FIVE When the silver clay is completely dry, it will easily tip out of the moulds.

STEP SIX It will help later on if the back of each button is flat. Place the dry buttons, back downwards, on to a piece of sandpaper and move them around gently in a figure of eight pattern until the back is smoothed.

STEP SEVEN Carefully work around the edges of the buttons with an emery board or a piece of sponge-backed sanding pad to smooth any rough edges.

STEP EIGHT Ensure the buttons are completely dry and fire by your chosen method and according to the manufacturer's instructions.

STEP NINE Brush the fired buttons firmly with a wire brush to bring up a matt silver shine.

STEP TEN Rub firmly over the surface of the buttons with a burnishing tool such as a crochet hook or knitting needle. This will bring up a bright shine.

STEP ELEVEN If you have the means to do so, you can solder the sterling silver cuff-link fittings on to the back of the buttons, but to keep things simple, you can secure the fitting with some extra-strong glue.

Copper-tube beads

Copper tubing is inexpensive and makes a great colour contrast with the silver. There are endless ways to decorate a simple piece of tube. As the silver shrinks slightly during the firing process, it grips firmly around the copper. This is a good project for using up scraps of silver clay.

MATERIALS

- 5g pack of silver metal clay
- Approx. 4in (10cm) copper tubing, approx. ⅛in (3mm) diameter
- Olive oil
- Playing cards
- Sandpaper
- Textured plastic sheet
- Roller
- Silver-clay paste
- Bucket
- Wire brush
- Silver chain with clasp

STEP ONE Cut the copper tube to lengths of approx. ¾in (2cm). Smooth over any rough edges using a piece of sandpaper.

STEP TWO Lightly grease a playing card, which will be your work surface. Roll out the clay to the thickness of four playing cards and press on a texture of your choice.

STEP THREE Using the edge of a playing card as a cutting tool, cut long, thin triangles in the clay.

STEP FOUR Wrap the triangles around the copper tubes carefully so that the ends just overlap. A little paste on the tip of the triangle will help it to stick. Dry thoroughly and fire the tube beads using your chosen method and according to the manufacturer's instructions. Because the silver clay shrinks slightly during the firing process, the outer silver layer will grip tightly on to the copper tube after firing.

STEP FIVE Drop the beads into a bucket of cold water the moment they come out of the kiln.

STEP SIX Brush the beads vigorously with a wire brush to remove any remaining black bits.

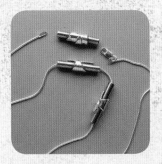

STEP SEVEN Thread the beads on to a silver chain to emphasize the contrast with the warm glow of the copper.

As soon as the beads are removed from the heat of the firing process, the copper part will quickly oxidize and turn black. The quickest and easiest way to remove this black layer is to drop the beads into a bucket of cold water, the second they are removed from the heat. The beads crackle and the black bits break off. Then remove the beads from the water.

Plain band ring

Making rings with silver metal clay is easy once you understand
how to adjust the size to allow for the shrinkage factor. A few helpful
tips will ensure your rings look good – and are a perfect fit!
This plain band ring looks elegant and can also be the basis
for many more exciting and exotic ring designs.

MATERIALS

- Finger-ring gauge (Japanese sizes)
- Ring mandrel (the round wooden stick to form your ring around)
- Sticky notepaper
- Pencil
- 7g pack of silver metal clay
- Roller
- Snake maker (a flat piece of glass or Perspex)
- 4 playing cards or ¹⁄₁₆in (1½mm) rolling strips
- Water spray
- Sharp blade or craft knife
- Crochet hook
- Sandpaper
- Fine-grade sponge-backed sanding pads
- Baby wipe
- Wire brush
- Polishing papers
- Burnishing tool

STEP ONE Silver clay shrinks slightly when fired; this method allows for shrinkage of approximately 10 per cent. Firstly, measure the finger on which the ring will be worn. This finger gauge, widely available from metal-clay stockists, shows Japanese sizes. The gauge should fit snugly over the knuckle but be comfortable around the base of the finger – this is the *finished* size. To calculate the size the ring should be made to, add three to the finished size; this is the *working* size. These instructions work best for a narrow to medium width of band. A wider band needs to be of a larger size even for the same finger. If you want to make a wide band, the working size will need to be four or even five (Japanese) sizes larger.

STEP TWO Wrap a sheet of sticky notepaper around the ring mandrel and then slide the finger gauge on to the stick, over the paper. Draw a line around the mandrel to correspond to the *working* size of your ring.

STEP THREE An average band ring will use about 7g of clay. Roll the clay into a thin 'snake'. It is difficult to do this with bare fingers so use a flat piece of glass or Perspex.

STEP FOUR Roll the snake flat, to a thickness of ¹⁄₁₆in (1.5mm). These rolling strips come in various colours to denote different thicknesses. Alternatively, use four playing cards. By now, you will have worked the clay quite a lot and you may notice tiny cracks appearing. To minimize further drying, lightly spray the surface with water, turn and repeat on the other side. Wait two or three minutes, until the water has been visibly absorbed.

STEP FIVE Wrap the strip of clay around the mandrel using the pencil line as a guide. The line should be in the centre of the band. Any deviation will result in the ring being either smaller or larger. When the clay strip is wrapped completely around the mandrel, there will be an area of overlap where one end of the strip lies on top of the other end. With a sharp blade, slice through both layers in the overlap area, at an angle to the mandrel.

STEP SIX You will now have two spare end pieces of clay that can be removed. The first piece will be on top of the band, and if you slightly unwrap the strip, the second piece will be on the inside.

STEP SEVEN Carefully re-wrap the strip. Because the cut ends are slightly tapered, one can be layered over the other, which makes a stronger join than butting two flat edges together.

STEP EIGHT Carefully blend and smooth the area over the join by adding a little water and working with a smooth-tipped tool such as a crochet hook. Work until the join is almost invisible; then dry the ring thoroughly.

STEP NINE Remove the ring and the paper from the mandrel. Carefully pull the paper away from the inside of the ring. The top and bottom edges of the ring can now be smoothed and flattened by gently moving the ring in a figure of eight pattern over a piece of sandpaper. Work very carefully at this stage since the ring is extremely fragile.

STEP TEN Put the ring back on to the mandrel and work over the outside of the band with a gentle abrasive such as a sponge-backed sanding pad.

STEP ELEVEN To smooth the inside of the ring and the 'corners' of the band, which can sometimes be a little sharp after sanding, gently wipe the ring over with a baby wipe. The dampness of the wipe is very effective at minimizing any roughness. Dry the ring thoroughly and fire by your chosen method and according to the manufacturer's instructions.

STEP TWELVE After firing, brush and burnish or polish the ring. Smooth, undecorated areas of silver look most professional when finished to a high, mirror shine. There are a number of ways to achieve this; here I used polishing papers to smooth and polish the surface of the ring to a bright finish but you could also use a burnishing tool.

hearts ring

Hearts ring

This adaptation of the simple band makes for a fun and romantic ring.
Any decorations that need to be evenly spaced around the ring are
best added when the band is set on the mandrel, otherwise you risk
losing the design when you make the join. You could save the cut-out
hearts for another project.

MATERIALS

- 7g pack of silver metal clay
- Ring mandrel (the round wooden stick to form your ring around)
- Finger-ring gauge (Japanese sizes)
- Sticky notepaper
- Pencil
- Roller
- Snake maker (a flat piece of glass or Perspex)
- 4 playing cards or ¹⁄₁₆in (1½mm) rolling strips
- Water spray
- Sharp blade or craft knife
- Crochet hook
- Very small metal cutter approximately ³⁄₁₆in (4mm) diameter
- Sandpaper
- Fine-grade sponge-backed sanding pads
- Baby wipe
- Wire brush
- Burnishing tool
- Polishing papers

STEP ONE See page 110 for directions on how to measure finger size and calculate the ring size. Mark the *working* size on to a sheet of sticky notepaper wrapped around the mandrel.

STEP TWO Using a roller, roll the clay on to a plastic sheet to form a 'snake' of the approximate length of your ring.

STEP THREE Roll the snake flat, to a thickness of ¹⁄₁₆in (1.5mm) – the thickness of four playing cards. Alternatively, use rolling strips, which come in various colours to denote different thicknesses. Spray the strip lightly with water to rehydrate the clay before proceeding. See band ring page 110 for more information.

STEP FOUR Wrap the strip of clay around the mandrel using the pencil line as a guide. The pencil line should be in the centre of the band. Any deviation to either side will result in the finished ring being either smaller or larger than planned. When the clay strip is wrapped completely around the mandrel, there will be a clear area of overlap where one end of the strip lies on top of the other. With a sharp blade, slice through both layers of clay in the overlap area, at an angle to the mandrel (see step 5 on page 110). Follow steps 6 and 7 on page 111.

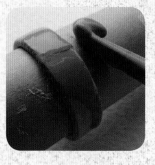

STEP FIVE Carefully blend and smooth the area over the join by adding a little water and working with a smooth-tipped tool such as a crochet hook. Work until the join is almost invisible; then dry the ring thoroughly.

STEP SIX Carefully cut out the hearts from around the ring band. Mark the paper with a pencil at even spaces as a guide to help you to space the hearts evenly around the ring.

STEP SEVEN Dry the ring thoroughly and carefully remove it from the mandrel.

STEP EIGHT The top and bottom edges of the ring can now be smoothed and flattened by gently moving the ring in a figure of eight pattern over a piece of sandpaper. Work very carefully at this stage since the ring is extremely fragile.

STEP NINE Put the ring back on to the mandrel and work over the outside of the band with a gentle abrasive such as a sponge-backed sanding pad.

STEP TEN To smooth the inside of the ring and the 'corners' of the band, which can sometimes be a little sharp after sanding, gently wipe the ring over with a baby wipe. Dry the ring thoroughly and fire by your chosen method and according to the manufacturer's instructions.

STEP ELEVEN After firing, brush and polish or burnish the ring in the usual way (see page 111).

Cocktail ring

This ring is a huge sparkler – in the true tradition of the fifties
cocktail ring! This project combines the techniques of ring making
and mould making plus an unusual way to include coloured gemstones.
Your ring could be symmetrical or abstract; there are no rules here,
so make your ring as large and colourful as you dare!

MATERIALS

- 15g pack of silver metal clay
- Two-part modelling compound
- A playing card
- An interesting button or other original object
- Selection of kiln-safe gemstones
- Emery board
- Finger-ring gauge (Japanese sizes)
- Ring mandrel (the round wooden stick to form your ring around)
- Sticky notepaper
- Pencil
- Roller
- Snake maker (a flat piece of glass or Perspex)
- 4 playing cards or ¹⁄₁₆in (1½mm) rolling strips
- Water spray
- Sharp blade or craft knife
- Crochet hook
- Sandpaper
- Fine-grade sponge-backed sanding pads
- Baby wipe
- Silver-clay paste
- Wire brush
- Burnishing tool
- Polishing papers

STEP ONE Make the mould from your original object or button. See moulded pendant (page 98) for detailed information on how to make a mould.

STEP TWO Place as many kiln-safe gemstones into the bottom of the mould as you can – the more the better!

STEP THREE Push the silver metal clay into the mould, being careful not to disturb the stones underneath. Dry thoroughly.

STEP FOUR When the clay is dry it will easily tip out of the mould. Smooth any rough edges with an emery board or sponge-backed sanding pad.

STEP FIVE Make a plain band ring. See band ring (pages 110–111) for the instructions. Paste the band ring on to the back of the moulded ring top. Dry thoroughly.

STEP SIX Fire the ring by your chosen method and according to the manufacturer's instructions. Allow the piece to cool slowly after firing.

STEP SEVEN Brush with a soft-bristled wire brush to reveal a lovely silver shine. A narrow brush with short bristles can be useful to polish the inside of the ring.

STEP EIGHT Using polishing papers polish the finished ring or use a burnisher to highlight parts of the design.

After firing, allow the ring to cool slowly as any sudden change in temperature may cause the stones to crack due to thermal shock.

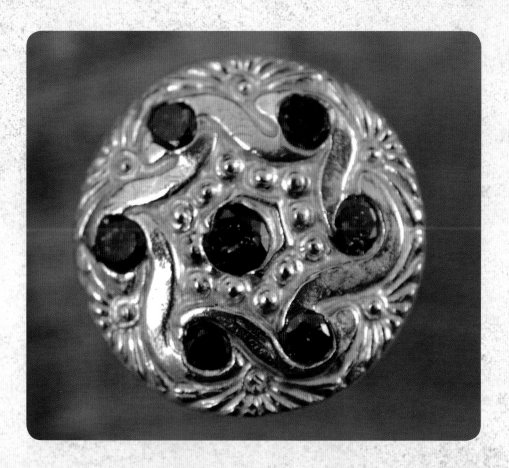

cocktail ring

Enamel pendant

Available in a huge variety of opaque and translucent shades, cold enamels are a great way to add colour to your designs. The cold enamels used here are added into recessed cells to produce the same colourful effect as traditional enamels. Unlike conventional enamels, these colours don't need to be heated in a kiln to fuse to the silver.

MATERIALS

- 2 x 7g packs of silver metal clay
- Playing cards
- Olive oil
- Roller
- Oblong cutter approx. 1½ x ¾in (4 x 2cm)
- Square cutter approx. ½in (1cm) diameter
- Water spray
- Small circle cutter approx. ¼in (5mm) diameter
- Sandpaper
- Wire brush
- Polishing papers
- Cold enamels suitable for painting glass or ceramics
- Cocktail sticks
- Piece of suede thong, ribbon or chain

STEP ONE Lightly grease a playing card with olive oil; this will be your work surface. On this card, roll 7g of clay to the thickness of four playing cards. Cut the first oblong from this clay. This will be the base of the pendant.

STEP TWO Repeat step one with the second 7g of clay, to form the upper layer of the pendant. Remove any excess clay and keep it for another project!

STEP THREE Cut three squares from the upper layer to create the cells for the enamel.

STEP FOUR Lightly mist the base oblong with water. This will ensure that the top layer adheres firmly to the base.

STEP FIVE Carefully lift the top layer from the playing card and place it directly on to the base oblong. Press gently until the two layers hold firmly together.

STEP SIX Using the small circle cutter, cut through both layers to make a hole to hang the pendant from. Dry the piece thoroughly.

To ensure the pendant stays flat, it may be necessary to turn the piece over several times during the drying process.

STEP SEVEN Carefully sand the edges to ensure they are flat and even. Fire the pendant by your chosen method and according to the manufacturer's instructions.

STEP EIGHT Brush the fired piece firmly with a wire brush to bring up a satiny, silver sheen.

STEP NINE This pendant looks good if the silver areas are really smooth and shiny to contrast with the opaque, coloured enamels. Therefore I have finished the polishing process by using consecutive grades of polishing papers to bring up a bright shine. It doesn't matter if the inside surface of the cells is rougher since it provides a better key for the colours to adhere to.

STEP TEN Carefully add the colours into the cells. I find it best to use a cocktail stick and add just a drop at a time. Ease the colour out to the corners with the tip of the stick. Allow to dry. The colour shrinks as it dries so it may be necessary to repeat this step to fill the cells. Allow 24 hours to dry completely. To ensure a permanent, glossy finish, the pendant can be baked in a domestic oven according to the enamel manufacturer's instructions. However, I have found my enamels to be very long-lasting even without baking.

STEP ELEVEN Finish the pendant with your choice of thong, ribbon or chain.

enamel pendant

Linked squares pendant

Liver of Sulphur is sometimes called Antiquing Solution and gives new silver an aged patina. This technique works especially well on areas of textured relief or raised detail because it creates a contrast between the raised and recessed areas. The solution is safe to work with but rather smelly and messy; using hard-boiled eggs is a cleaner, greener alternative!

MATERIALS

- 10g pack of silver metal clay
- Olive oil
- Playing cards
- Roller
- Sheet of textured plastic
- Square cutter approx. ¾in (2cm) diameter
- Emery board
- Wire brush
- Burnisher
- Liver of Sulphur and jam jar of hot water or two hard-boiled eggs and a clean plastic bag
- Silver polish
- Small hand drill or pin vise
- Pliers
- Jump rings
- Thong, ribbon or chain

STEP ONE Lightly oil a playing card; this will be your work surface. Roll 10g of clay between two stacks of five playing cards. Press the texture sheet firmly on to the clay.

STEP TWO Cut two squares, re-roll the clay and repeat step one to make one more textured square.

STEP THREE Thoroughly dry all three squares and then carefully smooth any rough edges or sharp corners with an emery board.

Liver of Sulphur is safe to work with, but it is very smelly. Always work in a well-ventilated area and dispose safely of any used solution.

STEP FOUR Fire the squares by your chosen method and in accordance with the manufacturer's instructions.

STEP FIVE Brush and burnish the squares.

STEP SIX Make the Liver of Sulphur solution by adding three or four drops from the bottle into a clean jam jar of hot water. Dip the first square into the solution. Within a few seconds, its surface will begin to change colour. You may see a range of colour changes from gold and green through blue and purple to almost black. Check every few seconds until you reach the colour you want, then rinse the square in clean water.

 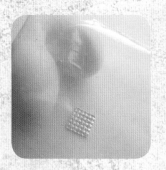  

STEP SEVEN Compare the square that has just been dipped in Liver of Sulphur with one that hasn't yet been treated.

STEP EIGHT If you don't have any Liver of Sulphur or prefer not to work with chemicals, you can achieve the same effect by sealing your piece of silver into a plastic bag with two peeled, hard-boiled eggs! Leave for about an hour or until the desired colour is achieved.

STEP NINE Compare the three squares: untreated, treated with Liver of Sulphur and after the hard-boiled egg treatment.

STEP TEN Rub the surface of the silver with silver polish. This will remove the colouration from the raised areas only. Rinse in clean water.

STEP ELEVEN You can see on the right-hand square how the treatment has darkened the recess areas of the pattern, contrasting with the raised areas.

STEP TWELVE Make holes for the jump rings with a small hand drill or pin vise and assemble the pendant using a thong, ribbon or chain.

3

Piped ring

This is another fun way to create a ring! Silver clay can be purchased in several different forms and here it comes supplied in a plastic syringe, ready to use. Piping directly from the syringe creates a random, spaghetti-like form, which you can decorate with coloured stones and tiny silver balls.

MATERIALS

- 10g pack of silver metal clay in a syringe
- Finger-ring gauge (Japanese sizes)
- Ring mandrel (the round wooden stick to form your ring around)
- Sticky notepaper
- Pencil
- Cocktail stick
- 5 x ⅛in (3mm) kiln-safe gemstones such as coloured cubic zirconia
- Sharp blade or craft knife
- Small amount of silver clay in 'lump' form
- Sandpaper
- Fine-grade sponge-backed sanding pads
- Baby wipe
- Wire brush
- Barrel polisher or burnishing tool

STEP ONE Measure your finger and set up the ring mandrel to the correct size. See band ring (page 98) for detailed information on how to size your ring and prepare the mandrel.

STEP TWO Holding the tip of the syringe above the paper, pipe around the mandrel in a random pattern.

STEP THREE Using a cocktail stick, gently push the stones into areas of the ring where the clay is slightly thicker, so that the widest part of the stones are fully embedded in clay.

Stand the syringe in water, tip downwards, when not in use.

STEP FOUR Make the tiny silver balls to add to the ring. Roll a small amount of clay into a thin snake and cut off little sections to roll into balls.

STEP FIVE Push the balls into the wet clay to decorate the ring. Dry the ring thoroughly.

STEP SIX Carefully remove the ring and the paper from the mandrel, then gently pull the paper away from the ring. The ring is fragile at this stage.

STEP SEVEN Inspect the ring for any sharp points or rough edges. Smooth these areas with a sponge-backed sanding pad and wipe the ring over with a baby wipe.

STEP EIGHT Fire the ring by your chosen method and according to the manufacturer's instructions.

STEP NINE Brush the ring with a wire brush. It is possible to get a lovely shine using a burnisher, but because of the fine lines of this ring, a barrel polisher is ideal to get into all those little, awkward spaces.

When you fire stones with the clay, allow the piece to cool slowly after firing. Any sudden change in temperature may cause the stones to crack.

piped ring

Stacking rings set

This modern set of stacking rings can be worn separately
or together, in any combination – according to your mood.
Plain or embellished, you can have fun decorating the rings with
a wide variety of techniques. This project introduces the skill
of carving dry clay and an unusual way to set a stone.

MATERIALS

- 10g pack of silver metal clay
- Ring mandrel (the round wooden stick to form your ring around)
- Finger-ring gauge (Japanese sizes)
- Sticky notepaper
- Pencil
- Roller
- Snake maker (a flat piece of glass or Perspex)
- 4 playing cards or ¹⁄₁₆in (1½mm) rolling strips
- Water spray
- Sharp blade or craft knife
- Crochet hook
- Sandpaper
- Fine-grade sponge-backed sanding pads
- Baby wipe
- Syringe
- Engraving tool
- Kiln-safe gemstone
- Modelling compound
- Small amount of 'lump' clay for decoration
- Wire brush
- Burnishing tool
- Polishing paper

STEP ONE Prepare the ring mandrel and mark in pencil the guideline for the centre of the rings set. Refer to the band ring (page 98) for more information on how to work out the correct size to make your ring. Because of the total height of the finished ring stack, I suggest making these rings a (Japanese) size or two larger than usual.

STEP TWO Roll 10g of silver clay into a sausage – not too long.

STEP THREE Flatten the sausage between rolling strips. Spray the clay lightly with water and allow this to be absorbed before continuing.

STEP FOUR Wrap the clay around the mandrel so the ends overlap, using the pencil line as a guide. The line should be in the centre of the band. Cut through both ends where they overlap; remove the two spare ends.

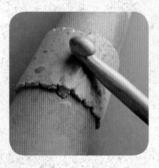

STEP FIVE Blend the join with a little water and the back of a crochet hook.

STEP SIX With a sharp blade, cut through the wet clay in a circle directly around the centre of the band. Then cut each of the resulting two bands in half to create four separate narrow-band rings. It doesn't matter if they are different widths.

STEP SEVEN Carefully remove the paper and the rings from the mandrel. Gently pull the paper away from the inside of the rings. The bands should separate. If they don't, the tip of a sharp craft knife should be enough to part them. Smooth the edges of all the bands by gently moving them over a piece of fine sandpaper.

STEP EIGHT Refine the outside of the bands with a sponge-backed sanding pad and a quick rub over with a baby wipe.

STEP NINE Now to decorate the rings! I've chosen a lovely pink cubic zirconia for the first band. Paste a small circle of fresh clay on to the band and press the stone into this. Using a syringe, carefully pipe two thin lines from the ring shank, across the stone and back to the shank on the other side. This makes an unusual but very secure setting for the stone.

STEP TEN This band has been patterned with a sharp engraving tool. Mark the pattern with pencil guidelines first. The other narrow band will be left with a plain, polished finish.

STEP ELEVEN This band has been decorated with two tiny leaves that were shaped in a mould. Refer to the moulded pendant (page 98) for more information on making and using moulds.

STEP TWELVE Dry all the rings thoroughly, then fire them by your chosen method and according to the manufacturer's instructions. After firing, brush and burnish or polish the rings.

stacking rings set

Gold pendant and earrings

This project explores the fascinating technique of Keum Bo,
which allows you to add real gold leaf to your fine silver designs.
The gold leaf is applied to the surface of the silver and gently heated
to form a permanent bond. Working with pure gold is incredibly
exciting and lifts your designs to a new level.

MATERIALS

- 10g pack of silver metal clay
- Olive oil
- Playing cards
- Square cutters approx. ¾in (2cm) and ½in (1cm)
- Heart cutter approx. ⅓in (8mm)
- Silver-clay paste
- 24-carat gold foil
- Greaseproof paper
- Pencil
- Sharp scissors
- Non-heat-conducting, cross-lock tweezers
- Metal pick with a wooden handle
- Heatproof surface
- Burnisher
- Wire brush
- Small hand drill or pin vise
- Pliers
- Jump rings
- Earring-hooks
- Chain

STEP ONE Lightly oil a playing card; this will be your work surface. Roll 10g of clay between two stacks of five playing cards. Cut two small squares for the earrings, a larger square for the pendant and three hearts. Remove the excess clay and save it.

STEP TWO Assemble the pendant and earrings by fixing the hearts on to the squares with a little silver-clay paste. Dry the three pieces thoroughly, then fire by your chosen method and in accordance with the manufacturer's instructions. Do not wire brush or polish the fired silver and keep all surfaces as clean as possible.

STEP THREE Sandwich the gold foil between two layers of greaseproof paper. Using the metal cutter as a template, draw on to the top layer with a pencil to use as a cutting guide. Cut out the hearts with very sharp scissors.

STEP FOUR The gold foil is applied to the silver with heat. Hold the silver piece in non-heat-conducting, cross-lock tweezers. Dip it into water and carefully position the gold-foil heart on top of the silver heart.

STEP FIVE Warm the silver over a medium gas flame, supported on a metal mesh. In the heat, the water will evaporate quickly and cease to hold the gold foil, so it can be helpful to gently hold it in place with a metal pick with a wooden handle.

STEP SIX As both metals heat, the gold foil will begin to stick to the silver. Touch the foil with a metal pick frequently to check on progress. As soon as the gold adheres to the silver, use the pick to tack down the foil, working from the centre outwards.

The temperature at which the gold fuses to the silver is well below the melting point of either silver or gold. So the heat required for Keum Bo is well below that required to fire silver. Moderate heat and pressure (burnishing) are the most important elements. I have found this technique to be most successful when heating the silver from underneath.

STEP SEVEN Remove the piece from the heat and working on a heatproof surface, quickly and firmly press the foil on to the hot silver with a clean burnishing tool. If it cools, heat again and continue. The gold will adhere to the base in a smooth, even layer. If the foil tears, don't worry; patch any tears with another small piece of foil by repeating the above process.

STEP EIGHT Repeat the gilding process for all three pieces then wire brush to reveal the silver – it's OK to brush over the gold. Continue to burnish or polish the silver.

STEP NINE Using a small hand drill or pin vise, drill the holes to hang the earrings and pendant.

STEP TEN Use pliers to add jump rings, earring-hooks and a chain to complete the set.

Silver flower moulded bead

Hollow beads are great for showy, focal centrepieces because
they are light and, by rolling the clay thinly, are not too expensive
to make. This project borrows a technique from pastry chefs and
introduces a neat trick for manipulating very thin sheets of clay.

MATERIALS

- 10g pack of silver metal clay
- Olive oil
- Playing cards
- Plastic mat
- Kitchen plastic wrap
- Roller
- Ready-made moulds
- Craft knife
- Sandpaper
- Pencil
- Round needle file
- Cocktail stick
- Silver-clay paste
- Sponge-backed sanding pad
- Wire brush
- Burnisher

STEP ONE Cover the plastic mat with a piece of plastic wrap and lightly grease the film. Cut the lump of clay into two pieces, save one half and roll the other between three playing cards, directly on the film. The resulting sheet of clay is very thin but the film makes it easy to pick up.

STEP TWO See moulded pendant on page 98 for detailed instructions on mould making. Carefully lower the sheet of clay into the mould. Gently but firmly press the clay into the mould, ensuring it reaches into all corners and indentations. Don't worry if the clay tears at this stage.

STEP THREE Trim any excess clay from the top of the mould with a sharp knife. Keep all the trimmings.

STEP FOUR Using the trimmings, patch any tears or thin areas inside the mould. It doesn't matter if this doesn't look pretty as it will be on the inside of the bead and no one will see it. Dry the clay in the mould.

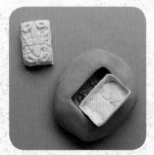

STEP FIVE When the clay is dry it will tip easily out of the mould. Do this carefully because the thin clay is now particularly delicate. Repeat steps 1–5 with the remaining 5g of clay to make the second half of the bead.

STEP SIX The edges of both halves now need to be filed until they are smooth and flat. The best way to do this is by placing one half on to a piece of sandpaper on a flat surface and gently moving and rotating the bead over the sandpaper. Then repeat with the other half.

STEP SEVEN Continue sanding and regularly check progress by holding the two halves together to see how they fit. Eventually, they will fit neatly together like two halves of a shell.

STEP EIGHT Mark with a pencil where you plan to make the bead hole. Mark both halves.

STEP NINE Using a round or semicircular file, gently draw the file over the pencil mark until a semicircle space has been created. Do this on the other half and then repeat the process to make the second hole.

STEP TEN With a cocktail stick, smear a thick layer of paste around the inside of one half – avoiding the hole area. Then fit the two halves together and place the bead somewhere safe to dry, with the pasted half on top. In this way, any paste that drips inside the bead shell will cover the join and make a secure bond.

STEP ELEVEN Inspect the area around the join. Any gaps or dents can be filled with paste, dried and filed again to create a smooth, imperceptible join. Dry thoroughly before firing.

A sponge-backed sanding pad is ideal for sanding the bead at this stage. The unfired clay is very delicate and a sanding pad, which can be cut to size, provides a gentle way to smooth over small areas.

STEP TWELVE The fired bead can be brushed and burnished or polished in the usual way.

silver flower moulded bead

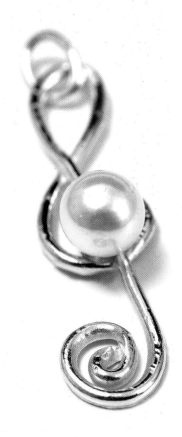

Treble-clef pendant

Once you gain confidence working with the syringe, it is easy to follow
a template to create figurative or filigree designs. This musically inspired
project will allow you to practise your technique and learn how to set
a beautiful pearl into your pendant. Any open design such as a leaf
or a flower would work equally well.

MATERIALS

- 10g pack of silver metal clay in a syringe
- Pen and paper
- Sticky tape
- Clear plastic sheet
- Plastic mat
- Fine silver wire approx. ½in (1cm) long
- Half-drilled pearl
- Paintbrush
- Sponge-backed sanding pad
- Small file or cocktail stick
- Wire brush
- Burnisher or barrel polisher
- Wire cutters
- Extra-strong glue
- Pliers
- Jump ring
- Chain

STEP ONE Trace a treble clef motif on to a piece of paper using the template opposite and tape this on to your work surface under a sheet of clear plastic or acetate. If you can rescue the clear plastic window from a packaging carton, it will be ideal for this project.

STEP TWO Check that the silver wire fits the drill hole on the pearl. If it doesn't, you may need a narrower gauge of wire.

STEP THREE Piping the clay directly from the syringe, trace the lines of the design directly on to the plastic sheet.

The best way to achieve a smooth line is to hold the tip of the syringe above the surface you are working on and lower the line of clay on to the surface, over the lines of the design.

STEP FOUR Carefully insert the piece of wire into the centre of the design. Use the tip of a wet paintbrush to gently smooth the clay and shape the lines. Allow the clay to dry completely. Once dry, the treble clef can be easily removed from the plastic sheet.

STEP FIVE Refine the shape and very gently smooth any rough edges with a sponge-backed sanding pad. Smooth the inside of the loop with a very small file or a cocktail stick.

STEP SIX Fire the pendant by your chosen method and in accordance with the manufacturer's instructions.

STEP SEVEN Carefully wire-brush and polish the fired pendant. It is possible to get a lovely shine using a burnisher, but because of the fine lines of this pendant, a barrel polisher is ideal to get into all those little, awkward spaces.

STEP EIGHT Trim the wire to the correct length for the drilled pearl. Apply a very small amount of extra-strong glue to the tip of the wire and push the pearl on to the wire.

STEP NINE Use pliers to fix a jump ring through the top of the pendant and hang on a fine chain.

TREBLE-CLEF TEMPLATE
100%

Two-part heirloom locket

A modern take on the traditional locket, this lovely pendant
contains a secret garden. In this project you will learn how to shape
clay to create a hollow form from two concave halves. The outside of
the locket is textured and the inside decorated with flowers and leaves.
Truly an heirloom for the future!

MATERIALS

- 10g pack of silver metal clay
- Olive oil
- Playing cards
- Plastic mat
- Roller
- Rubber stamp or texture sheet
- Large circle cutter approx. 1¼in (3cm) diameter
- Egg storage shelf or other round shape
- Sandpaper
- Metal file
- Pencil
- Small flower and leaf cutters approx. ¼in (½cm)
- Two eyelet loops
- Silver-clay paste
- Cocktail stick
- Plastic drinking straw
- Syringe
- Wire brush
- Burnisher or barrel polisher
- Pliers
- Jump ring
- Chain

STEP ONE Lightly oil a playing card to be your work surface. Cut 10g of silver metal clay in half and roll 5g between five playing cards. Texture the surface with an attractive stamp or a texture sheet.

STEP TWO Cut a large circle. This will be the front of the locket. Repeat this process without the texture; this will be the back of the locket. Collect the excess clay and save for later.

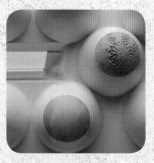

STEP THREE Drape the two circles over a domed form to create the concave halves. Here, I have used the back of an egg storage shelf from my fridge. If you don't have one, you could use a large marble, a doorknob or a table-tennis ball! Allow the clay to dry completely.

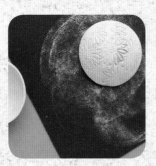

STEP FOUR Carefully move the two halves to your work surface. Working on a piece of fine sandpaper, gently move each half of the locket over the surface to smooth the edges. Hold the two halves together frequently while working to check they fit together snugly without any gaps.

STEP FIVE With a pencil, mark the exact spot on the edge of each half where the stem of the eyelet will sit. Gently file a small nick in this place with the metal file.

STEP SIX Roll the remaining clay from step one on to an oiled playing card, this time to the thickness of three playing cards. Cut two small flowers. Use a cocktail stick to apply silver-clay paste to the stems of the eyelet loops, then paste the flowers on to them. Fit the eyelet loops into the spaces created in step five.

STEP SEVEN Now for the fun part! Decorate the inside of the back half of the locket with a selection of leaves, flowers, or whatever you like. Roll the remaining clay to the thickness of three cards and paste the shapes into the locket.

STEP EIGHT Flower stems can be added with a syringe. Pencil the lines in first; it's easier to follow a line than to work freehand in a small space. Ensure both halves are completely dry. Fire by your chosen method and according to the manufacturer's instructions.

STEP NINE Wire-brush and polish the locket. It is possible to get a lovely shine using a burnisher, but because of the shape and detail in this locket, a barrel polisher is ideal to get into all those little, awkward spaces.

STEP TEN To emphasize the texture and detail, the locket has been lightly treated with a solution of Liver of Sulphur (see page 126).

You can pinch one side of a piece of plastic drinking straw to form a pear or leaf shape.

STEP ELEVEN
To make up the locket, use the pliers to fit a jump ring through both eyelet loops so that the two halves hang together. Thread on to a chain.

GLOSSARY

Agate burnisher A burnisher used to shine areas of fired silver and for applying gold leaf.

Antiquing solution Alternative name for Liver of Sulphur, used to created an aged patina on fired, polished silver.

Bail back A loop-shaped fixing, made from fine silver, which can be pasted on to the back of a pendant.

Barrel polisher A barrel filled with tiny pieces of stainless steel, which tumble around as the barrel rotates and polish the silver evenly.

Binder An organic binder, derived from wood pulp, which holds the silver together while in its pliable 'clay' state.

Burnish A simple process for polishing the surface of fired silver by rubbing it with a burnishing tool that has a harder surface than that of the silver, for example, another metal or a hard stone such as agate.

Emery board The type used by manicurists; very useful for refining dry clay.

Enamel Traditional enamel is ground glass that is fired on to the surface of the silver. In this book, I have used 'cold enamels', which are permanent paints of the kind used for decorating glass or porcelain.

Eyelet A small loop fixing suitable for pasting on to earrings or small pendants.

Findings A generic term for fixings and fittings such as brooch backs, hooks, loops or rings, which finish a piece of jewellery.

Fine silver Silver which is 99.9 per cent pure silver and can be hallmarked 999.

Finger-ring gauge A cardboard gauge to measure finger size. It is better to use Japanese sizes for silver-clay work as all materials and equipment for silver metal clay were developed in Japan. Adding three Japanese ring sizes is also the best way of anticipating shrinkage of the clay during firing.

Fire A generic term for the use of heat to transform the dry clay into silver metal. Silver metal clay can be fired in three different ways.

Firescale A black layer that can form on a metal containing copper when it is heated.

Found object Any locally sourced items which can be incorporated into the jewellery making process, such as buttons, shells or leaves.

Freeform An abstract, asymmetrical or irregular shape or design.

Gemstones In this book, any small, man-made coloured stones that can be pressed into the clay and fired as one.

Gold foil A wafer-thin leaf of pure gold – a relatively economical method of adding gold to silver designs.

Hallmark This word originates from the 15th century, when London craftsmen were first required to bring their wares to Goldsmiths' Hall for assaying and marking. Today it equates to a legally binding mark of quality and value.

Jump ring A small silver ring used to join two pieces of silver, such as in a bracelet or a pair of earrings.

Keum Bo An ancient Korean technique for applying gold leaf to fine silver using heat and pressure.

Kidney cutter A very thin, sharp cutter especially shaped for cutting curved lines.

Kiln A small, fast-heating oven suitable for firing metal clay. It is also known as a jewellery or enamelling kiln.

Kiln safe Refers to the man-made gemstones and fine silver fixings which can be safely fired with the clay by any method, not necessarily in a kiln.

Liver of Sulphur A chemical used to create an aged patina on fired, polished silver.

Mandrel A round, tapered stick for shaping rings.

Matt Unpolished areas of silver.

Metal mesh Used to support pieces while firing over a gas ring.

Modelling compound A two-part compound for making moulds, available from craft stores.

Mould A small shaped or patterned receptacle into which soft clay can be pressed so that it assumes the shape of the mould.

Pin vise A small, hand-held drill.

Polish A generic term for the many techniques which can be employed to bring a high shine to the surface of fired silver.

Polishing papers Papers containing graded particles, which are graded by colour and should be worked through in the correct order.

Polymer clay An inexpensive, plastic-based modelling clay available in a huge range of colours.

Roller A non-stick plastic roller for flattening lump clay.

Silver-clay paste Also known as slip, silver-clay paste is clay mixed with water to create a thick liquid which can be used to join two pieces of clay, for adding fixings and for decoration.

Snake maker A flat piece of Perspex for rolling thin coils of clay.

Sponge-backed sanding pad Sanding grits on a sponge backing, useful for gentle sanding and finishing.

Sterling silver Silver which is 92.5 per cent pure silver and can be hallmarked 925.

Syringe clay Silver clay supplied from the manufacturer in a plastic syringe, which can be piped directly from the syringe and is good for creating decorations.

Texture An effective surface decoration applied to the clay while in its pliable state.

Texture sheet or mat A patterned plastic or rubber sheet which can be pressed on to soft clay.

Tissue blade An extremely thin and sharp blade for cutting straight lines.

Torch A small kitchen or chef's gas torch used to fire silver clay.

Wire brush Small brush to reveal the silver metal after firing.

SUPPLIERS LIST

UK

www.cooksongold.com
PMC products, Art Clay Silver,
all jewellery supplies

www.fredaldous.co.uk
Wide selection of craft-based materials
including jewellery supplies

www.georgeweil.com
Art Clay Silver, polymer clay, tools
and accessories

www.metalclay.co.uk
Art Clay Silver, polymer clay, tools
and accessories

www.silverclayworkshop.co.uk
Art Clay Silver, tools, classes and
workshops

www.thesilvercorporation.co.uk
Comprehensive range of silver and
metal findings and jump rings

USA

www.artclayworld.com
Art Clay Silver information and
products

www.cooltools.us
PMC and Art Clay Silver products
and accessories

www.firemountaingems.com
Wide range of jewellery and beading
supplies

www.metalclaysupply.com
PMC and Art Clay Silver products
and accessories

www.thepmcstudio.com
PMC products and training courses

www.riogrande.com
Tools and equipment for the
professional and amateur jeweller

www.wholelottawhimsy.com
PMC and Art Clay Silver, accessories
and courses

AUSTRALIA

www.silverlab.com.au
Art Clay Silver information and
products

www.ceramicandcraft.com.au
PMC products and accessories

www.metalclay.com.au
PMC and Art Clay Silver products
and accessories

NEW ZEALAND

www.artclaynz.co.nz
Art Clay Silver information, products
and classes

USEFUL WEBSITES AND FURTHER READING

WEBSITES

www.artclaysociety.com and **http://pmcguild.com**
US-based societies for the promotion of metal clay.

www.artclayworld.com and **www.pmcguild.co.uk**
UK-based societies for the promotion of metal clay.

www.artinsilver.com
Hadar Jacobsen is an innovative and respected metal-clay artist.

www.honudream.com
Gordon K. Uyehara is an award-winning metal-clay artist with a distinctive style.

www.metalclayacademy.com
Comprehensive website with advice on how to find a teacher, international events and latest developments in the world of metal clays.

www.metalclayguru.com
Fun website with a learning library, tips and tricks section, galleries and information to enable you to achieve enlightenment on all things metal clay!

www.snagmetalsmith.org
Society of North American Goldsmiths.

www.thegoldsmiths.co.uk
Information on the requirement for gold and silver items created in the UK to be tested and hallmarked by an assay office.

BOOKS

Duhamel, Louise, *Metal Clay Jewelry*, (North Light Books, Iola, 2006)

Fago, Celie, *Keum-Boo on Silver*, (Vermont, 2004)

Haab, Sherri, *Metal Clay and Mixed Media Jewelry* (Watson-Guptill Publications, New York, 2007)

Heaser, Sue, *Magical Metal Clay Jewellery* (David & Charles, Newton Abbot, 2008)

McCreight, Tim, *Precious Metal Clay Techniques* (A&C Black, London, 2007)

Simon, Barbara Becker, *Metal Clay Beads* (Lark Books, Asheville, 2009)

MAGAZINES

Art Jewelry magazine
www.artjewelrymag.com
A wonderful magazine featuring news, advice, reviews, techniques and projects for traditionally constructed jewellery as well as metal clay projects. Also has inspirational gallery pages.

Making Jewellery magazine
www.makingjewellery.com
Loads of jewellery based projects, some of which feature silver clay. Fun interviews, reviews and tutorials on basic jewellery making techniques.

Metal Clay Artist Magazine
www.metalclayartistmag.com
The only print publication in the world devoted entirely to metal clay. Features articles and tutorials from the leading artists and teachers working in metal clay around the world.

Ornament magazine
www.ornamentmagazine.com
Unique magazine featuring traditional and modern jewellery plus a variety of personal adornment crafts.

ABOUT THE AUTHOR

MELANIE BLAIKIE'S love of all things sparkly began when she trained as a diamond valuer for De Beers. She went on to forge a successful career as a jewellery designer – working for many of the biggest names in the industry, including Garrard, Asprey and Tiffany. After studying traditional silversmithing techniques, Melanie discovered silver clay and fell in love with this amazing medium. She is now one of the foremost tutors of silver clay work in the UK and regularly contributes to *Beads and Beyond* magazine.

INDEX

**To place an order
or to request a catalogue, contact:**

GMC Publications, Castle Place, 166 High Street,
Lewes, East Sussex BN7 1XU United Kingdom
Tel: +44 (0)1273 488005 **Fax:** +44 (0)1273 402866
www.gmcbooks.com